OCCULT EXERCISES AND PRACTICES

A non-technical guide to general principles of spiritual development through the techniques of occultism in the form of physical, astral, mental and spiritual exercises, with an appendix on psychic self-defence.

OCCULT
EXERCISES
AND PRACTICES

Gateways to the Four 'Worlds' of Occultism

GARETH KNIGHT

SUNCHALICE BOOKS
1997

This edition revised and reset 1997.

Published by
SUN CHALICE BOOKS
PO Box 9703
Albuquerque, New Mexico
USA 87119

Copyright © 1997 by Gareth Knight

All rights reserved. No part of this book may be reproduced or transmitted in any form or by any means, electronic or mechanical, including photocopying, recording or by any information storage system without written permission from the publisher except for the inclusion of brief quotations in a review.

Publisher's Cataloging-in-publication Data
Knight, Gareth
    Occult exercises and practices / Gareth Knight
    p.   cm.
    Includes index
    1. Occultism
2. Spiritual life   I. Title
BR115.O3 K   1997   200
ISBN 0-9650839-6-9
    (previous edition published by Aquarian Press, ISBN 0-85030-296)

Cover design by Nicholas Whitehead

Contents

The Four 'Worlds' of Occultism 7

Physical Exercises 11

Astral Exercises 33

Mental Exercises 57

Spiritual Exercises 71

Appendix: psychic self-defence 81

Index 89

CHAPTER ONE

THE FOUR 'WORLDS' OF OCCULTISM

Systems of spiritual development through the techniques of occultism are many and various and it is not wise to mix systems. However, it is often very difficult as a student to decide just which is the way for you amongst all the varying methods and teachers, whether Eastern or Western. For only one will be the way for you and it is your task to find it.

There are, however, basic similarities between the various systems and this book is written with the idea of putting forward the general practical principles which you can use prior to pursuing your studies to a deeper level under the system of your choice.

All the paths lead to the same goal but in the initial and intermediate stages they differ in their symbolism, and the emphasis which they place on various aspects or levels of development.

Four 'Worlds'

The exercises are divided into four chapters in accordance with the four 'worlds' that the occultist recognizes. These are the *Physical World*, which includes the etheric, or vital stress systems which hold the physical world together; the *Astral World*, which is the world of the imagination and where most magical work (as the term is generally understood), is done; the higher *Mental World* of the intuition where the basic techniques are concerned with meditation; and the *Spiritual World*, which is the world of archetypes, basic principles and the contemplations of faith.

Each of these worlds is equally holy and each needs to be developed by the intending occult adept who is eventually to become worthy of the name, and it is unfortunate that some occult schools place too much emphasis on one end of the scale or the other.

Those who value the physical and astral end incline to a form of psychism and magic which, although at its best is useful for certain purposes such as healing or divination, is not spiritually directed or informed with intuitional insight. At the other end, those who overvalue the spiritual and mental tend to be highly idealistic and of impeccable principles but lacking in any magical attainment.

Those who consider themselves to be extremely 'spiritual' often do not realize that the spiritual plane can be as open to evil and folly as the mental, astral or physical planes, and this is usually demonstrated by the extreme self-righteousness, exclusiveness and sectarianism of such people or groups — who tend to regard themselves as 'more evolved' than their lesser brethren. But in reality they are as much in error as those opposite extremists who can only think in terms of getting something for nothing by sorcery or thaumaturgy.

Biblically speaking we have the occult Pharisees on the one hand and the occult Simon Maguses on the

The Four 'Worlds'

other. Both types by their running to extremes are, in the main, ineffectual rather than potent for good or evil, for the occult way is the middle way and equal development on all the planes is essential for effective action.

To avoid the frequent assumption that the so-called higher levels are superior to the lower levels, we commence our exercises with the physical plane and work our way upwards.

The physical plane is the one upon which our consciousness is initially centered as we are today and we have spent a great many years of our childhood and adolescence in attaining a balanced control of this plane. It should therefore be our jumping off point, for to open up objective awareness on other planes will merely increase our confusion if we have not mastered the physical plane.

Another common cause of error in occultism is the insufficient distinction between the subjective and the objective and it is possible to go a very long way in occult development without getting any closer to union with God — which is, after all, the whole end as well as the beginning of our existence.

You may, as you open up the inner faculties, become more aware of your subjective depths which lie beneath everyday consciousness, like the vast mass that exists beneath the visible tip of the iceberg. You may even achieve at-one-ment with the 'god-within' but this is not necessarily the same thing as achieving awareness of — and cooperation with — the denizens of the inner planes, nor with coming to a personal relationship with the Living God.

OCCULT EXERCISES AND PRACTICES

CHAPTER TWO

PHYSICAL EXERCISES

Relaxation is an important part of any occult work, for the inner senses cannot be used correctly while there is psychological tension, whether it be conscious or unconscious.

The mind is closely connected with the physical body and you will find that an intentional and systematic relaxation of the body will relax the inner tensions and thus make the way ready for useful inner activities.

The first thing to do is to lie down on a hard surface. The fact that it is a hard surface will serve to accentuate the fact, in no uncertain manner, if you are not fully relaxed. Take a few deep breaths, rather in the manner of sighs, and then proceed to deliberately relax the body, muscle by muscle.

It is a good idea to start at the head and work slowly downwards, mentally commanding each muscle to relax in turn. And then, when you have gone through the whole body, return to the head again and see if any muscles have tensed up again. The whole body should be gone through like this several times until there is no unconscious tensioning.

It can help to visualize the blood pouring into muscles which are reluctant to relax, feeling this fresh red oxygenated blood washing away all strain and fatigue poisons and bringing healthy poised relaxation. Work from above downwards, for tensions are dropped, and it can be an aid to imagine the tensions and strains streaming from the tips of the fingers and from the feet and toes.

The test of relaxation is that if someone lifts one of your limbs it should fall back limply. If you have no helper, a good physical way to ensure relaxation of the limbs is to lift each one very slowly — try to do it as slowly as possible — and then let it fall back to the resting position under the force of gravity.

Breathing

Breathing exercises form a large part of certain types of occultism, particularly in the East. The ability to breath deeply and correctly in a rhythmic fashion is important to occultism although some of the more complicated techniques should be avoided at this stage.

Rhythmical breathing will improve the powers of relaxation, help to still and concentrate the mind as a basis for visualization and meditational work, and also result in beneficial physical effects, in that we tend to use our lungs inadequately most of the time.

The main thing in breathing technique is not to strain, particularly by constriction of the throat. There must be no forced effort. The air should be taken in to the bottom of the lungs first, by the simple method of pushing the abdomen out (i.e. the diaphragm down) and thus causing the air to be sucked naturally into the lungs until they are filled to the top. Be conscious of the air passing up and down the upper throat rather than through the nasal passages – this will prove more occultly effective.

The air should be retained for the requisite time by holding the diaphragm down and the chest wall out, and if the chest is tapped sharply it should cause part of the air to be expelled, thus proving that there is no barrier in the throat or mouth.

To breathe out, suck the abdomen in (i.e., the diaphragm up), so that the air is dispelled naturally and is felt to leave the top of the lungs last of all. Keep the breath held out by use of the diaphragm and trunk muscles.

The Four-fold Breath

For general purposes the four-fold breath is the most useful. That is, inhale slowly to a count of eight; retain the breath to a count of four; exhale to a count of eight; and hold the lungs empty to a count of four. The speed of counting should be according to individual preference.

It is most important to avoid strain or 'overbreathing' which will give symptoms of dizziness.

Rhythmic breathing can be done while relaxed as part of the physical exercise, or at any time of the day in almost any attitude, perhaps while out walking. It will also be used to advantage prior to any of the mental and imaginative exercises to be described later.

Properly done, it will result in a general feeling of well-being, with the whole body seeming to vibrate with beneficent power. The sensation is unmistakable once it is experienced – though it must *be* a sensation.

OCCULT EXERCISES AND PRACTICES

These relaxation and breathing exercises are basic to all practical occultism and should be sedulously practiced, not only as the foundation for all future work, but for their own sake and the physiological benefits that will accrue.

Note: *Relaxation and rhythmic breathing should be done prior to most of the exercises outlined in this book. It is most important before starting any occult work to have your system working rhythmically and smoothly.*

Sense Awareness

In occult work we are dealing much of the time with images in the imagination and the majority of these images come from experience of daily life. Your inner work will therefore be the better if you have used your physical senses to the full. Practice really looking at things as a child does. Fully appreciate color, feelings, texture, shape, weight and smell.

This is not an intellectual process, in fact the intellect should remain dormant. It is a simple being aware of something and using the powers of physical observation to the full. This will enrich your imagination to a very great degree.

It is very easy to fall into clichés of observation. In answer to the question, 'What are the colors of the leaves on that tree?' do not say simply 'Green.' Go out and observe a tree and see the many different shades of green and the many other colors therein. Go also to look at the sky, particularly at dawn and dusk, for a real appreciation of color. Many of the colors of the objective astral plane have no physical counterpart, save only in these radiant forms of physical color.

Having No Head

An extension of developing sense awareness uncluttered by intellectual preconceptions is to be found in a technique known to its advocates as 'having no head.' It was discovered by Douglas Harding, who has written a short book on it, originally published by the Buddhist Society of London, entitled *On Having No Head: A Contribution to Zen in the West.*

There are various methods of inducing this state of awareness, which seems to come easier to younger people, although they generally seem to find it less remarkable an experience than the middle-aged or elderly, who have developed a crust of preconceptions about things and themselves over the years, and who therefore may find a great sense of release and vividness of perception not experienced since early childhood.

It is best introduced at one of the experiential sessions called 'workshops' by someone who is already 'opened' to it but it is by no means impossible to develop it yourself. It is a question simply of rejecting all preconceptions about oneself as an object in an alien world and looking at the world of experience as a subjective entity. This brings about a realization that the world of perceptions about you only exists because *you* are conscious of it. *You* are *yourself* the whole world. All that exists is in *you*. *You* are constantly creating it.

This philosophical position is not attained by thinking about it, for it transcends 'objective' thought. It is realized by the simple act of forgetting your face, regarding it as a hole in space. Imagine your face as non-existent, a peephole through which you see the universe. If walking along, or riding in a car, see the road as disappearing into yourself as you move. In-

OCCULT EXERCISES AND PRACTICES

deed, see the road and the countryside moving into and around a stable you. You are the stable, constant 'nothingness' about which the phenomenal world appears.

The experience can often be induced by pointing your finger at the opposite wall as you sit in a room and registering what you see. Then bring the pointing finger downwards across the floor towards your feet. From the feet continue pointing the finger up the legs, up the trunk, and then, just above the breast bone, register exactly what you see. If you say 'my face,' that is mental speculation, hearsay information provided by others, exactly what you want to avoid. On the only real authority, your own experience, there is nothing to be seen when the pointing finger rises higher than the breast bone. You see the finger pointing into a void.

Although this may sound ridiculous according to our accustomed conventions of thought, to experience it is another matter, and it is perhaps the quickest way to an experience of 'Zen' that there is.

Postures

Eastern occultism goes in for some very complex postures but in the West all occult work can be performed by the four basic simple postures of lying, sitting, kneeling and standing. Each of these is appropriate to various activities. Standing for practical ritual work; sitting for meditative work; kneeling for prayer; and lying for certain types of astral travel or inner communication.

Each one should suggest its own appropriateness to the student who is at all sensitive and has some sense of esoteric propriety. All that need be said about them

Physical Exercises

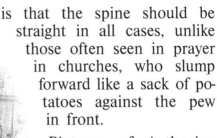

is that the spine should be straight in all cases, unlike those often seen in prayer in churches, who slump forward like a sack of potatoes against the pew in front.

Pictures of Arthurian knights kneeling at their vigil as portrayed by Victorian artists show the type of posture for kneeling. The Egyptian gods show the best kind of sitting posture, with the forearms along the thighs, which should be level, the feet square upon the ground, with a footstool under them if necessary for comfort in keeping the knees together.

In the lying position it is usually best to clasp the hands over the solar plexus. In the standing position a poised position should be aimed at, usually best achieved by placing one foot at right angles immediately behind the other, and holding the hands palm to palm, the fingers pointing straight upwards, with slight pressure being maintained from the forearms, held horizontally before you. Comfort and alert poise are the watchwords in all these positions.

OCCULT EXERCISES AND PRACTICES

Generally speaking, to close the aura, which is best for most subjective work, the ankles can be crossed and the hands clasped. To open the aura, that is, to transmit or to receive energy, the feet should be uncrossed and the hands unclasped. The hands placed to the sides and slightly back give extra reception; pointing with a finger gives projection; holding forth the palm of the hand gives radiation.

Some of the simpler yoga exercises are excellent purely as physical conditioners and these can readily be obtained from any simple introductory text on the subject. They help to keep the spine supple and the spine is an important channel of occult forces. Exercises involving complex contortions, however, or intricate breathing exercises, should not be pursued by the majority of Western students.

Model Making

The use of the hands is an important and often underestimated adjunct of occult training and it is a very good principle for anyone who pursues the higher knowledge also to practice some handicraft in order to maintain integration on all levels.

On the emotional and mental levels too, the appreciation of one of the arts will keep the emotions lively

A three-dimensional model of a three-ring system, such as is descibed in *The Cosmic Doctrine*, can be made of strips of card.

Physical Exercises

and the pursuit of some stiff mental discipline such as chess, bridge, mathematics or logic will make the mind tough and resilient.

The lack of these precautions accounts for much of the slushy sentimentality and woollymindedness that is regrettably common to the fringes of real occultism. For similar reasons the occultist should also cultivate normal family and social relationships to the full; there is no place in it for the type of misfit who regards personal idiosyncrasies as a badge of superiority over the rest of the human race

Again, keen interest in non-occult subjects will bring social relationships that provide a balanced personality — and it is easy to become unbalanced in the pursuit of the subject at its deeper levels. Fortunately the weaker and naturally unstable types of personality rarely have the ability to get to these deeper levels.

The hands and fingers have a wisdom of their own which can only be experienced by setting them to work on certain esoteric lines. Personal ingenuity should suggest objects to make, but, as an example, three-dimensional models out of card are easily made without a long training, and will be found to increase your understanding immeasurably, far more than notebook jottings and two-dimensional drawings.

Models can be made of various cosmological concepts put forward in various occult textbooks, such as Dion Fortune's *Cosmic Doctrine*. Three-dimensional models of esoteric symbols such as the Tree of Life

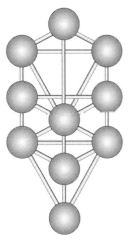

Tree of Life

can also be made out of pieces of wire and balls of modeling clay. Or you could make a model of the castle of the Holy Grail or of a ritual temple — either as described in a book or from your own imagination. The opportunities are endless.

The Platonic Solids

The Platonic Solids are models worth making, as they comprise important principles of esoteric thought and symbolism, and they are simply constructed out of card. They are five in number† and have been regarded as important representation of universal principles since the ancient Mystery school of Pythagoras. They are:

 the **tetrahedron**, (4 triangular faces), which represents the Element of Fire;

 the **octahedron,** (8 triangular faces), which represents the Element of Air;

 the **cube,** (6 square faces), which represents the Element of Earth;

 the **icosahedron**, (20 triangular faces), which represents the Element of Water;

 the **dodecahedron** (12 pentagonal faces), which represents the Spirit or Universal Principle ruling the Elements.

†Modern mathematics has discovered three more, but they are simply decorative embellishments of three of the basic five.

The Elements

The five-fold symbolism of one over four is an important principle of esoteric philosophy, as it represents spirit over four-fold Elemental matter, and is to be found in the Pentagram, the five pointed star which is a magical symbol for banishing unwanted forces and exerting the magician's spiritual will.† It is also the central rose on the Rose Cross, and indeed the central balancing point of any *mandala* (or fourfold meditational figure which forms an important part of Jungian psychology).

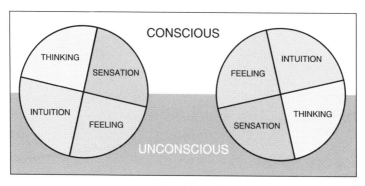

Jungian Mandalas

The Elemental forces may also be held to represent aspects of consciousness:

Air - the intuition and aspirations;
Fire - the intellect and thought processes;
Earth - the physical senses and sphere of sensation;
Water - the feelings and emotions.

†For a description of the Pentagram ritual see *The Practice of Ritual Magic* by Gareth Knight (Sun Chalice Books)

The Platonic Solids can be made of appropriately colored card or painted in bright poster colors. We would suggest red for Fire, yellow for Air, blue for Water, and green for Earth. These are commonly regarded as the 'active' colors for each. You could also experiment by coloring another set of Platonic Solids in the 'passive' colors, of crimson, azure, silver and russet-brown. Or try the effect of combining active and passive colors on different faces. Or else experiment with the Tattva colors.

The dodecahedron, representing spirit, or a universal synthesis, could have twelve colors, one for each facet (the colors of the spectrum split into twelve shades and taken from red to indigo is a useful formula), and perhaps allocated to the twelve signs of the Zodiac.

The complete figures will give much scope for meditation, in the number, configuration and relationship of their sides, edges and corners.

Elemental Modeling

Modeling in Elemental materials is also a useful exercise in extending consciousness in unfamiliar ways, and can be very therapeutic occupational therapy.

Modeling in clay is a particularly earthy and stabilizing exercise. It is not often recognized that one can model in water, but although the material does not retain its shape, 'water play' is loved by children and there is something very restful to the emotions in trailing one's hand in moving or still water. Rather than leave all the fun to the children, get to know the Element of Water (and your own emotions) by playing with it.

The same principle goes for Air and here one is almost into the realms of the dance; making passes

Physical Exercises

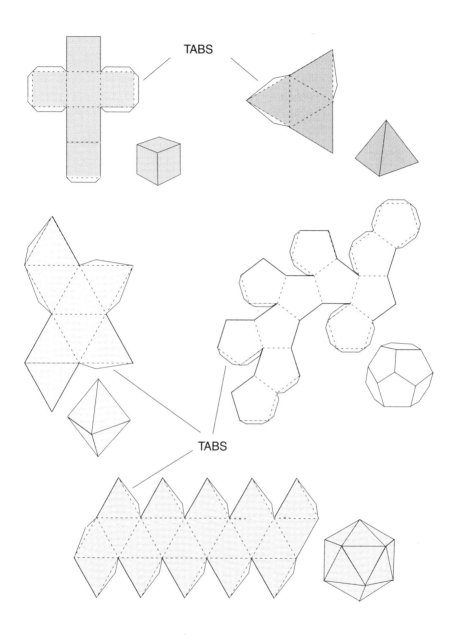

These nets for the Platonic Solids can be enlarged and copied on cardstock or heavy paper; then cut out, scored and folded along the dotted lines; and finally pasted at the tabs.

OCCULT EXERCISES AND PRACTICES

and gestures in the air can bring about a realization of a whole new world of meaning and experience. You do not have to be a ballet dancer to learn the language of movement and bodily posture, which has a wisdom and means of communication all of its own.

Modeling with fire is an extension of this, just as children love to brandish glowing brands from a garden bonfire, or firework sparklers, in the dark. An incense stick is an excellent 'fire pencil' to use for drawing glowing patterns in the dark or twilight.

Acting With Intention

The ordinary activities of daily life can be used to help your occult and spiritual development. Every outer action can be consciously worked on inner levels also.

For instance, when you bathe or wash, do so with intention also of cleansing yourself of your errors, impurities or sins. When you eat, do so with the intention of taking in the good things of life. Grace said before meals can be part of this intention rather than the empty formality it often is.

Likewise with the biological functions of excretion you can consciously reject all effete matter of the soul. Such exercises as these prepare the way for technique in ritual working and indeed, when fully understood and practiced, are the supreme form of ritual magic for they are the practice of the twenty-four hour ritual of daily life.

At times of stress, when all seems to be going wrong or getting out of control, a simple exercise of successfully acting with intention can prove very helpful.

Stand at one side of the room and *locate* a point of easy access on the opposite wall. *Decide* to walk across the room and touch it. *Do* so. Then turn and *identify* a similar arbitrary point of *your* choice on the wall you have just left. *Decide* to walk across and touch it. *Do* so. Then turn and repeat as before, for a number of times, until you feel thoroughly calm and in control.

Fatuously simple though this exercise may appear, it is highly effective in that it puts you into a situation you *can* control, and from this you gain the strength and confidence to return to the original difficult situation with renewed will, strength and sense of proportion.

Pore Breathing

When doing breathing exercises you can imagine that you are breathing not only with the lungs through the nose and throat, but breathing with your whole body through the pores. Imagine the breath passing in and out of your whole body. The sensation will be unmistakable.

You can also isolate certain parts of your body, such as the hands, or solar plexus, and imagine breathing taking place through there. This can in fact be done through any part of the anatomy — the stomach, the liver, the eyes, and so on. Such exercises should be done with caution, certainly at first. They lead the way to the control of astral and etheric forces within the aura (which is the basis of practical magic), and also to the practice of healing.

In ordinary breathing you can tie in this exercise with the one above; as you breathe in imagine good forces coming in and as you breathe out visualize the unwanted things within yourself flowing forth.

If you wish to imagine this in terms of colored light,

OCCULT EXERCISES AND PRACTICES

do so; it is a practice leading towards the techniques of astral visualization. Of course you do not have to visualize the outgoing breath as carrying waste and unwanted products; in certain operations of magic one becomes the mediator for spiritual forces and then the outgoing breath, which can be directed, is felt to be full of healing or other beneficial qualities.

Etheric Vision

The easiest way to develop the faculty of etheric sight, which does not come naturally to all of us, is to try to see auras. This is best done in the first instance by going out into the fields and trying it with trees, although it can be done indoors with pot plants. The more vital their growth the better, and a wet flannel with sprouting ears of wheat on it will probably be better than an ancient and slow moving cactus or succulent.

The technique is very simple. Simply look towards the object but not exactly at it, slightly defocusing the eyes, and after a time you will see an aura of color round the living object. Practice this with various objects, as soon as facility is achieved, in an endeavor to discern the extent and varying colors of the auras around different objects.

If this exercise does not easily produce results, a quickening exercise can be to practice the vision of complementary colors. That is, take a small piece of brightly colored paper and gaze at it intently and then after a minute or so gaze at a light-colored or white surface and one will see the shape come up in the complementary color. This should not be pursued to the extent of giving eye strain but will be found useful if done in moderation, particularly just before trying

Physical Exercises

to use etheric vision (The sections below on *Tattvas* and *Flashing Tablets* deal with an extension of this technique).

Another way of seeing the etheric is to put your two hands before a dark space, say in a drawer or cupboard, with the finger tips touching. Draw the hands slowly apart and streams of white etheric light will be seen streaming from one to the other of each finger. Move your hands and fingers about to see how the etheric flow is affected.

Having performed the previous experiment, it is possible to work at this by means of the imagination and will, gradually solidifying and strengthening these rays into what have been called 'rigid rays.'

You can then attempt minor physical phenomena such as floating a matchstick in a glass of water and attempting to etherically manipulate its direction of drift, or piercing a drinking straw with a needle in a cork so it turns very easily, and then trying to rotate it by means of the rigid rays.

Tattvas

One of the leading occult schools of the late nineteenth century, the Hermetic Order of the Golden Dawn, used what was originally an Eastern system of elemental attributions for inducing etheric vision. This was the attribution of the four elements, plus a higher fifth element, or aether, to five colored geometric shapes:

      a yellow square   for Earth
      a blue circle   for Air
      a red triangle   for Fire

OCCULT EXERCISES AND PRACTICES

a white or silver crescent for Water
a black oval for Aether (or Spirit)

Note that the color symbolism in this Eastern system varies slightly from the system described on page 22. One of the lessons you will need to learn in occult symbol systems is that no system is the 'one and only true.' Learn to work flexibly with any of them.

Now we use the well known 'optical illusion' of the after-image. Stare at any of the symbols for a minute or so and then gaze at a blank surface. You will see an image of the shape you have just been staring at, but in its complementary color.

This is not etheric vision but approximates the feeling of it and is a basis for developing it and also for externalizing vividly imagined objects. You can then go on to slightly more complex figures by superimposing the Tattva symbols one upon the other. There are twenty possible combinations. Make all the combinations in poster paints or colored paper. Air of Earth, for example, consists of a small blue circle superimposed on a large yellow square. The complete list is as follows:

Air of Earth: blue circle on yellow square
Fire of Earth: red triangle on yellow square
Water of Earth: white crescent on yellow square
Aether of Earth: black oval on yellow square
Earth of Air: yellow square on blue circle
Fire of Air: red triangle on blue circle

Physical Exercises

Water of Air: white crescent on blue circle
Aether of Air: black oval on blue circle
Earth of Fire: yellow square on red triangle
Air of Fire: blue circle on red triangle
Water of Fire: white crescent on red triangle
Aether of Fire: black oval on red triangle
Earth of Water: yellow square on white crescent
Air of Water: blue circle on white crescent
Fire of Water: red triangle on white crescent
Aether of Water: black oval on white crescent
Earth of Aether: yellow square on black oval
Air of Aether: blue circle on black oval
Fire of Aether: red triangle on black oval
Water of Aether: white crescent on black oval

The Elements in their pure essence, Fire of Fire, Water of Water, etc., are of course represented by their plain symbol, thus giving twenty-five symbols in all. These can be used as a basis for etheric vision training and also as contemplation on the results of combining elemental principles.

Flashing Tablets

Having achieved facility with the Tattva cards, you may go on to make some Flashing Tablets. These are abstract designs, or representational pictures, solely made up of two complementary colors. The complementary colors are:

OCCULT EXERCISES AND PRACTICES

red	and green
blue	and orange
yellow	and mauve
black	and white

The optical principle involved is that as the after-image induced by any color is its complementary, a picture that consists entirely of two complementary colors will appear in the after-image state with the same two colors reversed out.

Not only that, but the nearer the colors are to being true complementaries, and the more intricate the intertwining of the color elements in the design, the more readily will the picture confuse the physical eye mechanism and the picture will appear to 'flash.'

This is a feature that is deliberately sought in what is known as Op-art; and can also happen with the printed word in certain circumstances, making the text difficult to read because of the 'flashing' property.

In its esoteric training function it can be used for the preliminary development of etheric vision. If, when practicing with Flashing Tablets, staring at them and then producing an after-image on another surface, you feel a tingling in the center of your forehead, this is the awakening of the 'third eye,' or *ajna* center, one of the psychic centers or *chakras* in the etheric body. Do not overdo this exercise; if overindulged in, it can lead to a painful headache, but regard it as an encouraging indicator that progress is being made and a warning not to try to develop too quickly.

Physical Phenomena

Much interest was aroused by Uri Geller and his technique of bending and breaking forks and other metal objects, simply by stroking them with intention. Much controversy resulted as to whether this was done by conjuring or not, it being claimed that Uri Geller was an experienced stage illusionist.

Whatever the merits of the case, and whether or not other stage illusionists can appear to produce similar phenomena by sleight of hand, it is remarkable to note that a number of children succeeded in emulating the feat, simply by believing in it and trying it! If faith can move mountains it can presumably bend forks. The problem for most intelligent modern adults is achieving sufficient strength and purity of faith.

Other types of phenomena seem possible and equally pointless and random. A little Italian girl could turn tennis balls inside out – a feat which defies the physical laws of nature anyway, let alone the additional fact that the internal vacuum was retained. She lost interest (and the ability to do it) when she reached puberty.

All of which simply goes to show that there are stranger things in heaven and earth than are dreamed of in our philosophy – and you never know *what you can do* until you sincerely try!

OCCULT EXERCISES AND PRACTICES

CHAPTER THREE

ASTRAL EXERCISES

There should always be a clearly defined beginning and end to any psychic or occult work, for it is important that the subconscious or psychic phenomena do not break in to consciousness in an uncontrolled fashion at any time of night or day. Should this happen regularly you should stop any psychic work for at least three months. Such lack of control can be avoided, however, by use of opening and closing signs, which are simply the hygiene of occult work.

The sign, rite or ritual can be as simple or complex as you like to make it, but for the simple nature of these exercises a straightforward sign should suffice, such as either the sign of the cross or a gesture of opening or closing curtains, or these signs in conjunction. Another sign is to stamp the foot hard on the ground after an experiment as a sign that the psychic faculties are closed.

At another level it will be found that a warm drink and something to eat will effectively close down the psychic faculties, and similarly of course it is a good idea not to have eaten or drunk immediately prior to psychic experiments.

OCCULT EXERCISES AND PRACTICES

A phrase or mantram can also be used in opening or closing. This need only be a statement of intention, such as 'I open the veil' or 'I close the veil.' Names of power and ritual evocation are similar devices but more highly powered, with built-in emotion and intention, and are beyond the scope of this work, although their intention and mechanics are exactly the same.

Concentration

A first requisite of occult work is the ability to concentrate well. In later work you will find that the astral imagery is so interesting that concentration is very easy to achieve, in fact you achieve it unconsciously. However, you must not be only a 'fair weather worker' but should be able to concentrate at will or make the screen of consciousness a blank, free from intruding images and thoughts.

The best way to do this is to relax and — after some breathing exercises — think of one particular object such as a tennis ball, or a complex one such as a board of chessmen. Whichever you find easier should be dealt with first, then progress to the harder.

When you have attained facility in holding the object steadily in your mind for ten minutes at least, practice dissolving the image of the object until nothing is there, and then just hold the nothingness in your mind. Again practice until you can do it easily for at least ten minutes.

If intruding images, sounds or thoughts persist in coming into consciousness, banish them with a sharp word uttered aloud or to yourself, such as 'No!' or 'Go!' Persistence in this simplest form of banishing ritual will soon prove its worth.

Visualization

All astral work is done by means of the imagination. This is primarily the visual imagination but includes also the auditory — and even the imagined senses of touch, feel, taste and smell. The best way to achieve facility is of course practice, and a good way is to imagine going for a walk, seeing and sensing all that is about you. This should be prefaced by the usual relaxation and breathing exercises, *which should be performed before attempting any of the exercises detailed in this chapter.*

You can imagine going for a walk around your house or out of doors. It is best to begin with scenes which are familiar; proceed to things remembered from past experiences; then to scenes from works of fiction; and eventually to scenes made up in your imagination.

Eventually you will be able to start with a particular occult symbol — such as a Tarot card — enter into the picture and then see what scenes or persons arise before you.

Two techniques are involved in all this: first, the active visualization whereby you put things in the imagination by an act of will, and you are thus the complete controller; second, where you allow images to arise spontaneously and see what they do. From this exercise, which is of fundamental importance, most astral occultism develops naturally.

The Guide Meditation

A development of visualization technique is Edwin Steinbrecher's *Guide Meditation*, which he describes fully in his book of the same name. In this you commence by imagining yourself entering into a cave

OCCULT EXERCISES AND PRACTICES

as intensely as you can. Then you imagine a doorway in the left-hand wall of the cave, which you go through. This turns to the right and leads to an exit. You wait there, observing the imaginary scenery which may arise spontaneously to your mind's eye. An animal of some kind should then come to you and you follow it wherever it leads you. It will bring you to a meeting with a person who, you will find, can act as a useful guide.

All characters visualized in this or similar exercises should be fictional. In fact, most of such images are projections of aspects of your own consciousness, and it will be confusing and unhelpful to use actual people as hooks for these projections.

You should ask the Guide his name, observe all items of his appearance as closely as you can, and ask him to take you to meet the Sun archetype. This is the symbol for the center and nucleus of your own being, and may result in a deep and moving experience, possibly of a religious nature. Allow it to take the form that appears spontaneously but if some form of visual prop is needed think of the Tarot Trump, the Sun. This is a smiling sun disc shining down, either upon two naked male children dancing in a fairy ring, or alternatively, upon a naked male child on a horse, carrying a banner.

At the conclusion of this exercise, and indeed any exercise of this nature involving imaginary venturing, retrace your steps back the way you came, and bring consciousness back deliberately to earth from the imaginative point from whence you started, in this case, just outside the cave.

Warning: In all inner contacts of this kind use common sense and a sense of proportion. Such techniques are capable of opening up access to deep areas of wisdom within your own consciousness but can lead the unstable, the credulous or the vainglorious into considerable folly and self-deception. It has been known for those who seek or take inner advice on material things such as gambling or playing the stock market to receive a hard financial lesson. On the other hand, rightly used, these techniques can be integrating and helpful in dealing with the problems of daily life. Similarly, any messages to the world at large, or teaching, should be very closely scrutinized in the light of skeptical common sense. Some very deep and abstruse teaching has been received by these methods but equally a large amount of platitudinous moralizing from shallow areas of the unconscious mind. These do no harm but if taken too seriously and portentously by those who receive them, can make the would-be amanuensis of the higher wisdom, and the subject as a whole, rightfully look absurd.

Developing Atmospheres

This is a development from the pore breathing exercises of page 25. Imagine you are breathing in power from the universe and transmuting it into a particular mood by breathing it out into a particular space, such as a room one is in. As an aid to this, various colors and occult symbols (usually planetary or zodiacal) may be used.

As a simple example, imagine yourself emanating bright golden light until it fills the entire room, at the same time feeling healing power and loving warmth emanating from you. With practice the resulting atmosphere should be easily discernible to any person who comes into the room, particularly if they are reasonably sensitive.

This is the use of Solar symbolism, which has a

OCCULT EXERCISES AND PRACTICES

good balancing all-purpose function, the sun being center and source of light, warmth and life for the whole solar system and thus a fitting living symbol for the central creative point of consciousness.

Traditional planetary attributions which may be used for experiment are:

Golden - Sun - general well-being, health, encouragement.

Purple - Moon - psychic perception; intuitiveness; healing atmosphere; pregnancy; growing things; tides.

Orange - Mercury - intellectual activity; good communication; business; travel.

Green - Venus - good feelings; harmonious relationships; love.

Red - Mars - activity; initiative; analysis; debate; justice; ending things.

Blue - Jupiter - stability; organization; respect for law; constitutional authority.

Indigo - Saturn (sometimes visualized with points of light like stars) - physical conditions; limitations; laws; money; property; ownership; consolation of grief; deep wisdom.

This type of work can also be done at a distance and is the modus operandi of certain types of absent healing. It is also the method of charging objects such as jewels or talismans with force, in which case you hold the object in the hand and concentrate on pore breathing through the hand.

Control of Mood

As in our visualization exercises we have learned to construct a 'composition of place,' so can we construct a composition of mood, which of course is closely connected with the previous exercise. By building a series of symbols which you associate with particular moods, you can then induce the mood in yourself by visualizing the symbol. This can be very useful in daily life when you are subjected to various shocks and distractions.

One can also make up one's own system of physical signs to go with moods, such as finger positions, which of course can be done without drawing curious attention to yourself in everyday activities.

Finger Positions and Symbolic Gestures

Finger positions may seem a strangely ineffective way of achieving anything but if you have worked assiduously at some of the modeling exercises and realized the significance of ritualized actions, their potential may become apparent. In Eastern dance and yoga, hand and finger positions are highly important and developed to a considerable degree of subtlety.

On a less elevated plane, though embodying the same principle, think of the office boy carpeted by the boss, keeping his spirits up by having his fingers crossed. In a more truculent mode his equilibrium might well be maintained by a covert use of finger gestures of some considerable disrespect!

All this is a particular development of 'body language,' which has recently become recognized as an important factor in communication. Whatever we may be saying outwardly, our body may, by its attitude, be expressing contrary opinions or emotions. An actor's manual is worth perusing in this regard. It will detail what emotions are expressed by particular physiological reactions, be it the raising of eyebrows, the gritting of teeth, the flaring of nostrils, part closing the eyes, or opening them wide.

As St. Teresa said of prayer, by assuming the physical attitude the desire to pray will result. Sales training organizations have made similar injunctions to their trainees — act enthusiastically and you will become enthusiastic and thus overcome depression or negative thoughts about failing to make a sale. In other words, the appropriate physical posture can induce any particular emotion.

This principle is commonly utilized in occult practice as a prelude to meditation, to get into the right mood, either by the sign of the cross, to stabilize the emotions and currents of the aura, or by the Sign of the Enterer, which is a gesture that mimes the opening of curtains before passing through them. Likewise the coming down to earth at the end of a meditation may be confirmed by clapping the hands or stamping the foot on the floor.

Olfactory Suggestion

The composition of mood can be strongly influenced by the sense of smell. This is exploited by the use of incense in some churches, though a whiff of garlic from the pew behind can equally effectively dispel the induced feeling of piety. Similarly French perfume or unwashed linen can have powerful if differently emotive reactions.

For meditational purposes a general incense is certainly a great help, although it does tend to cling to clothes and to penetrate other rooms of the house, which may not always be welcome.

It is possible, by personal experimentation, to develop a battery of incenses, or types of joss stick, to suit particular types of meditation. Purveyors of meditational or magical accessories tend to have a range to choose from and experimentation along these lines can be an interesting pursuit. Or you may wish to develop your own incenses by collecting wood gums, chippings, leaves or flowers from nature. The country lore which will be absorbed in the endeavor will prove a rewarding and enriching adjunct to your esoteric activities.

Gustatory Suggestion

This is an area similar to that of olfactory suggestion, the sense of taste being closely akin to that of smell, and is another interesting field for experiment. Different tastes can be as mood inducing as different smells. Again, personal experiment is better than following a printed listing. Bread, wine, mint, salt, sugar, water, fruits, fungi, all have their particular association through taste, texture and context.

The Art of Memory

The art of memory is largely a lost one with the advent of cheap writing materials, printed books and the increase of literacy. In former days it was a highly cultivated art, particularly by public speakers, and by a technique that is largely 'astral' or one of visual images.

A speaker would have in mind a well-known street or building, and along or around it would place, in his

OCCULT EXERCISES AND PRACTICES

imagination, objects representing points he wished to cover in his speech. From this technique was developed the turn of phrase 'In the first place.,' 'In the second place ...,' etc.

Thus, supposing you wished to remember a shopping list, you could visualize each item in a different place as you imagined entering your house. In the porchway a packet of sugar, hanging on the doorknocker a string of sausages, on the hall mat a bowl of breakfast cereal, on the umbrella stand an umbrella made of cheese, the stairs made of chunks of pineapple, and so on.

The more ludicrous, bizarre or unusual the juxtaposition of objects and places the better, as they stay in the mind the more readily. In setting this up a clear, vivid visualization is all that is necessary — attempts at verbalization, or mnemonics of other kinds, are counterproductive. Having this clearly visualized set scene which you can go through in sequence, a long list of objects can not only be memorized but memorized in order, or in backward order.

The method is capable of considerable sophistication, so that lists of 100 or even 1000 items can be remembered in or out of sequence. See, for instance, Harry Lorayne's famous *How to Develop A Super-Power Memory*, in which he describes the basis for his most spectacular stage act.

This can be emulated by anyone who is prepared to put in the practice but it is interesting to note that a common reaction to hearing about this method is to say that it sounds too involved and fantastic to work. Yet it only has to be tried to be proven! It is an odd fact about many esoteric exercises and practices: they seem odd or illogical according to current common sense so people's first (and often last) reaction is to reject them, even where proof can be simply obtained by practice.

Recalling Sleep Experiences

It is a tradition amongst occult students that the soul continues in considerable activity during the hours of bodily sleep but that we do not normally recall this activity.

A way of developing continuing consciousness in sleeping and waking that was taught by the experienced and much-loved magician, the late W.E. Butler, is to construct a symbol chain.

Before falling asleep imagine that you are standing before a pylon gate of stone; that is, two massive upright stones with another laid across the top of them, rather like the trilithons of Stonehenge and other ancient stone circles. Between the two upright stones visualize a multicolored veil. This is divided in the center. Grasp, in the imagination, each half of the veil with your hands before your heart and then throw them open by extending the hands and arms sideways. In esoteric fraternities this is called the 'Sign of the Enterer.'

See a desert landscape before you with, in the near distance, a temple within a high-walled enclosure. Proceed towards it and enter the enclosure, which you should see to be a garden. Do not enter the temple building itself but remain seated in the garden. Try to fall asleep with this situational imagery in mind, combined with the intention of returning to everyday consciousness, after sleep, through the pylon gate.

Success in such an experiment will depend upon persistent endeavor, and, like most such astral experiments, success will come sooner to some than to others. It is a perfectly safe technique but should be used with discretion as maintaining continuity of consciousness in this way can prove tiring.

An Experiment with Time

This is a similar sleep experiment, and can also prove tiring if persisted in over too long a period. It is fully described by its inventor, W. J. Dunne, in a book of the same name. Dunne's theory was that we dream in the future as well as in the past. Therefore he advocated the experiment of writing down all one's dreams, even the most fragmentary, immediately upon waking. To delay in writing them down causes many of them to be lost to memory, so a writing pad by the bed is a necessity. With practice the facility at recalling dreams also improves.

You should then analyze these dream fragments to elicit how much of them contain images that are memories of the recent past; that is, the previous day or two. Dunne found that some people came up with images that were part of daily life not of a day or two before, but of the day or two after. In other words, part of our dreams are 'memories' of the future!

Dunne formulated a theory of time based on the results of his experiment, in which he put forward ideas of what he called a 'serial universe.' This is not too easy to understand unless one has a mathematical and philosophical bent but the experimental evidence can be gained by any individual who is willing to devote the time and effort to it, with a mind uncluttered by prejudice.

Identification

This exercise is to identify yourself with an object. Try to transfer your consciousness to the central point of the object and then feel what it is like to be that object.

You can commence with an inanimate object such as a table or a computer and progress to living things, such as flowers, trees, and even animals and people. In all astral work however, never try to identify with or project force onto a specific person without their full permission and knowledge of the issues involved.

Identification in this manner is again a preparation for advanced techniques of invocation in group ritual work when an officer identifies with the archetypal Messenger, Guardian, Hierophant, and so on, or with a particular god form.

This exercise is also a preparation for types of astral projection wherein you identify with an idealized image of yourself which you have projected in your imagination. Legends of warlocks and witches turning into certain animals are possibly vestiges of a particular use of this type of exercise.

At its highest level it can be an identification in daily life with Christ, an example of where prayer and occult exercise come close together.

Psychic Development

Most psychic development techniques are different means of communicating with your subconscious mind and much of the results obtained will have their origin in the subconscious. However the subconscious is the means of communication for the superconscious mind and external intelligences. Therefore, although much

OCCULT EXERCISES AND PRACTICES

matter of little worth may be obtained at first, the techniques do have importance for those who are gifted enough to develop them, but it needs commonsense and discernment to use them intelligently. Beware of casual use of psychic techniques and always act with deliberate intention of opening and closing these faculties. Sloppy and undisciplined use of them can turn them from useful servants into wayward masters.

Crystal Gazing

An actual crystal can be extremely expensive if a high quality one is desired, but any reflecting surface such as a bottle full of ink is equally serviceable. If a crystal is used place it against a black background.

The technique is to sit in front of the crystal, about twelve inches from it, with a shaded light in the room. Look steadily at the crystal without straining. Your mind should be blank during this process, your eyes neither fixed on any part of the ball, nor staring vacantly, nor yet wandering away from it or attempting to see into its interior. It is quite in order for your eyes to blink as in normal circumstances. If they start to water you should rest from the experiment.

Before any visions appear it usually happens that a dark gray mist will seem to fill the ball or to come between it and your eyes

Perseverance is necessary, the sitting being conducted daily at the same time. Five to ten minutes should be sufficient on each occasion.

Shell Hearing

This is a similar technique to crystal gazing, except

Astral Exercises

that the auditory faculty is used. It is well known that if a shell — or indeed any hollow object — is placed to the ear, a kind of rushing noise will be heard. This can be done to both ears at the same time, although not essential.

Practice regularly and for a few minutes at a time, listening to this type of sound effect from a shell or shells, or similar objects, and see if in time you can discern any voice communication.

Dowsing

A well-known form of dowsing is the use of a hazel wand or similar instrument to psychically detect water or hidden minerals. The term is also used, however, for work with a pendulum and gifted people are able to find things with a pendulum and a map. The pendulum can be any simple weight, perhaps a personal object such as a ring, on the end of a thread. Despite (or perhaps because of) its simplicity, the pendulum is a very good means of communication with and through the subconscious.

It is necessary to think up a simple code, such as straight swings for 'Yes' and circular swings for 'No,' or you could have clockwise and anticlockwise swings meaning different things. An alternative is to hang the pendulum in the mouth of a glass so that if it swings it will tap the glass and the number of taps can then spell out numbers or letters to an agreed code.

There should be no conscious attempt to swing the pendulum and it should be held still (the elbow resting upon the table usually). Of course the actual movements do not come from outside but from fractional movements of the arm caused by the automatic nervous system, by-passing consciousness.

OCCULT EXERCISES AND PRACTICES

Some operators address their subconscious with questions, giving it a name, such as 'George,' and coming to quite a friendly relationship with it.

The Ouija Board
This is a device with a purpose similar to that of the pendulum, except that several people can use it at once. It usually consists of an upturned glass on a smooth table with letters of the alphabet spaced around, with extra spaces for 'Yes,' 'No,' and 'Doubtful.' Each person present places the crossed middle and index finger of one hand on the glass and after while it will start to move about. Questions are asked of it and replies recorded.

This is probably the most popular 'dabblers delight' and is often performed in a spirit of party frivolity. Needless to say, the results usually reflect the circumstances. But it should not be despised as it is a legitimate form of experiment for all that. In so far as it is a group method, it can yield more interesting results than may be individually obtained, for more 'power' and 'subconscious content' is available as a pool of inner resources to work through and with.

Automatic Writing
This is another method of receiving communications via the subconscious. Sit in a semi-darkened room in a comfortable position with your mind kept as open as possible, a pencil held lightly in your hand. It is a useful refinement to imagine the etheric or astral counterpart of the hand and forearm as separating from the physical. And if you puts your mind in a receptive frame with a clearly expressed intention to receive guidance and wisdom, after a time your hand

may begin to write.

In the case of gifted experts the rate of writing is extremely rapid and many sheets of paper are quickly covered with intelligent communication. For the beginner, however, progress may be slow, and much nonsense or even scribble may be the result of the initial attempts.

A group method of automatic writing is possible by using the planchette, which is a usually heart-shaped device with two wheels, one at each cheek of the heart, and a pencil protruding near the point. The hands are placed lightly on the body of the planchette and communication awaited.

Telepathy

Telepathic experiments need at least two people to perform them; one should agree to be the transmitter and the other the recipient — though the roles can be reversed for separate experiments. They should sit apart, the transmitter imagining a simple geometric shape. It may help to draw the shape on paper in order to gaze at it intently. The transmitter should not strain in the effort of sending the image.

Concentration plus confidence is the thing to aim at, and it is usually best to imagine that the recipient has already received the message. The recipient makes his mind blank and notes down any pictures or impressions that come to him.

Success will probably not come easily, though some may find they have a gift for it. The early experiments should be with simple geometric designs; after success has been achieved with these you can go on to more complex images.

Telepathic messages do not have to be visual, of

OCCULT EXERCISES AND PRACTICES

course. They can also be in the form of spoken words, emotions and moods, or impulses to perform some action. Telepathy is an important part of occult work and is more common than is often realized nowadays. There is also a higher form of telepathy which works on an intuition-to-intuition contact. This is the technique used in certain advanced forms of occult communication between inner and outer plane adepts and this is developed more by the mental level of methods to be described later.

Psychometry
This is the faculty of picking up psychic impressions from physical objects; skilled practitioners can tell many things in the personal history of the object and of those connected with it. It is really a question of developing the facility to express first impressions, however absurd they may seem; a byword of psychic work is that the first ridiculous impression is the truth and the reasonable second thoughts are one's own imagination!

Apart from this, certain exercises can be undertaken, such as having a bowl of water at body temperature and lowering the fingers towards it with the eyes shut, until you can discern the approach and when your fingers are immersed. This is by no means as easy as it may sound if the temperature is correct.

Another exercise is to make identical packets of different pieces of metal such as iron, zinc, copper, brass, and so on, and to practice identifying them. You can also attempt the same thing with pieces of differently colored card or paper. An advanced form of this exercise is to be able to identify correctly at a distance.

Astral Exercises

Influencing Events

Things can be attracted to you by a combination of clear creative visualization and the harnessing of desire. To this end various techniques can be used, such as the making up of phrases affirming what you want, the cultivation of the firm confidence that you already have the object of desire or that the event has already happened. A physical help is a chart which has a border drawn all round it, and pictures within of what you wish to gain.

It is important that you do not show this indiscriminately to others — it is a tool for assisting in visualization and the stimulation of desire, and ultimately a simple form of talismanic magic.

Self-Projection

Strictly speaking there are two types of self-projection — etheric and astral. The first, in which you travel in the etheric and see the physical plane or its etheric counterpart, and the second where you project into your imaginative body and become aware of the objective astral plane.

Etheric Projection

Etheric projection is the more difficult, and can be attempted by going over the whole body in the imagination, willing that the etheric counterpart of each part becomes detached or loosened until you get a sense of separation taking place. Then imagine rising from your body and going to a particular physical location.

This is best done by attempting progress in a step-

OCCULT EXERCISES AND PRACTICES

by-step manner as if still bound by the conditions of the physical body, rather than trying to go there extremely rapidly — or instantaneously. Should you feel you are losing consciousness, discontinue the experiment by willing to return to the physical body.

A strong thread may be seen attaching the etheric vehicle to your physical body. This is a veritable life line, but do not concentrate on it too much as it will tend to drag you back forcibly to the physical body — although this is no bad thing in an emergency.

Astral Projection

Astral projection can best be achieved by picturing your self in the imagination and building this up with steady practice. A full length mirror may be used as an aid, or you can *imagine* an idealized figure. Drawing or painting it would help the imagination, if you have the artistic skill (Do not show the picture to others, though). Then attempt to transfer consciousness from the physical body to the figure projected in the imagination.

Another method — which some find easier — is not to bother with building an astral simulacrum but simply to step out of the physical body in the astral body — which of course you are already in, naturally and all the time! This can best be done by building up a pylon gate or doorway in the imagination (two side pillars and an overhead lintel are the important points), and then feeling yourself walking through it. Again, regular practice is necessary for good results.

Self-hypnosis

By self-hypnosis you can achieve improvements to yourself more effectively than by auto-suggestion. A good light hypnotic trance can be induced by use of a metronome, putting it on a shelf just above eye-level, with the weight at the top of the moving arm and covered with silver foil to make it bright. Now relax, gaze at it, and set it going with the prior intention of such a trance lasting for a specified time, such as twenty minutes.

You can then give instructions to your subconscious. These can take the form of instructing it to react post-hypnotically to certain images. For instance, you could instruct that if in the circumstances of daily life you should deliberately visualize a tiger, then on such an occasion you will not feel fear but rather be welling up with self-confidence and courage.

Such instructions as are to be given should be worked out well beforehand and not given until after some time of giving yourself instructions to fall into a sleep. Such instructions can of course be prerecorded on a tape recorder.

No weird and wonderful effects should be expected of the trance, simply a feeling of well-being and deep relaxation.

Recalling Past Lives

The following exercise is a modern technique for which we are indebted to Mr. William Swygard of *Awareness Techniques*, Massachusetts.

A very similar technique, though requiring the cooperation of another person, is described by G.M. Glaskin in his book *Windows of the Mind*, together with accounts of results of the experiment. Its application to other areas of investigation has been described in a book entitled *Explorations of Consciousness*, written by a group of scientists and edited by Dennis Milner.

OCCULT EXERCISES AND PRACTICES

First of all relax completely and then imagine yourself a few inches taller by stretching out through the soles of the feet. After a few seconds go back to normal size and then repeat, becoming a foot longer. Repeat this process again but becoming taller through the head and then extend yourself completely, as if blowing up like a balloon. Go back to normal size and repeat until facility is achieved.

When this comes easily, blow up like a balloon again in the imagination and see yourself at a particular building you know, outside it. Describe what you see in detail as regards the physical attributes of the building. Then go quickly to the roof and look down. Describe what is to be seen.

If the scene is daylight, turn it to night time and see what difference this makes; or if it is night time turn it to daylight, describing the difference this makes. Change it back and forth two or three times but conclude with having it daylight on a bright sunny day. Be certain that it is you that is causing it to be night or day.

Now will yourself, still high in the air, to return to earth, and as you come down to go back in time until, when you stand on the ground you are in a previous life. When the ground is reached look down at your feet and describe what you are wearing on your feet, and then all that you are wearing from the legs upwards. Then continue describing what you see and experience. This describing can be done either to another person or to a tape recorder.

It is permissible to work two or three lives through at a session, though one should obviously not overstrain. As a further experiment one can experience dying in a particular life and following through the death scene to what happens after death. This is quite safe and the only uncomfortable effects will be the emotional upset of death if it is a violent one.

The validity of these experiments can be tested by running through the same life on a later occasion after a period of time, when, if it is valid, you will come up with the same details or with details which do not conflict, whereas if it is fantasy or imagination there would obviously be discrepancies.

OCCULT EXERCISES AND PRACTICES

CHAPTER FOUR

MENTAL EXERCISES

Much that we have been concerned with in the last chapter has come under the province of what is sometimes known as the 'lower psychism' and it is not to be despised for all that, although unfortunately some esotericists tend to do so. It is true that much of it is more in the nature of parlor tricks or side tracks but this does not outweigh the advantages that it can have.

Apart from the value that it may have in its own right, some kind of carrot is needed at times for the donkey who essays the long path of occult development. The most important exercise in the development of higher psychism, or seership is meditation, but this can seem very boring and without apparent results for some time.

We should also say that certain of the astral exercises such as those concerning breathing and the circulation of force within the aura are dropped from the curriculum of occult schools to their great detriment, for it is in these exercises that magical power lies and there seems little point in being full of the

OCCULT EXERCISES AND PRACTICES

light of the higher wisdom but impotent to do very much occultly about it.

Meditation

There are various forms of meditation and the exercises which are known as meditations in the church are more properly called forms of prayer. The technique with which we are concerned is that of holding an idea in the mind and following trains of thought from it, but not in such a way that one is led far away from the original subject. The mind should be brought back to the main idea as soon as it begins to drift too far away.

Thus the mind circles round and round a key idea and in the process will bore a 'well' down through the layers of the concrete mind until, if persistently pursued, a breakthrough is made to the intuitional mental levels.

Through constant meditation on occult and religious symbols throughout the centuries there is a pool of intuitional wisdom which can be tapped (and contributed to) by the student. In this way wisdom may be gained without recourse to verbal or written instruction.

Naturally, this level of ability cannot be attained without diligent practice over a period of time, possibly several years, and the method can grow wearisome until such time as its worth becomes self-evident through personal experience. Eventually the well so bored into consciousness can become deep and wide enough for the technique no longer to be pursued as a daily discipline, for the higher wisdom becomes readily available simply by turning the mind in the right direction.

In Eastern terminology this is known as the building

of the *antakarana* between the concrete and abstract mind (or intuition), the Rainbow Bridge of Wisdom between the worlds, which is symbolized in Scandinavian mythology.

In the beginning, however, the student must content himself with following association chains stemming from the original meditation subject and should not expect any spectacular flashes of psychic imagery or intuition. The fact that the realizations obtained seem little different from the ideas that one might ordinarily expect to have had should not act as a discouragement. Realizations will become deeper until they are realization in the true sense of the world, and not simply ideas.

A realization is an idea or awareness that has been taken into consciousness — made *real* — so that it becomes an actual part of one's fund of experience and not a mere passing ripple on the stream of consciousness.

Midday Salutation

An ancillary exercise in making contact with higher consciousness is to try to attain an automatic state of recollection at a specific hour of the day. After a time you should be able to come to this state of recollection automatically at the right time, whether you have a watch or not, and under whatever distracting circumstances. As the quest of occultism is the quest of light, naturally the time chosen is midday, or if a particular zone time is used, the hour when the sun is highest in the heavens.

At first you may find that you forget this exercise very easily but this is all part of learning it. Essentially it is very simple. At noon simply look up to the sun and mentally salute God and the whole creation. You can at the same time visualize some astral sign such as a glowing flame in your heart corresponding to the physical sun of our solar system, or a sign of the cross forming within you.

This is entirely according to your choice. The important thing is the regular recollection and performance, on time, of this exercise, which takes but a few seconds and can be performed under virtually any circumstances.

The Cube of Space

This is an exercise which you can use in conjunction with the Midday Salutation but which is valuable in its own right for use at any time. It is an orientation of your self and if you have studied Jungian psychology you will recognize that it is in fact a three-dimensional mandala. It is also the mental basis for a great part of the rationale of ceremonial magic.

Simply imagine yourself at the center of a cube, which can be any size, even so large as to encompass the whole of space. And see each facet of the cube as an aspect of God. Thus you could almost make a small litany of 'God before me, God behind me, God on my right, God on my left, God above me, God below me, God within me' — the last point being the very center of the cube which coincides with the space occupied with your own heart.

This self orientation can be rendered more potent by realizing various attributes of God at each facet. Thus God Above is the God you look up to; God Below is the God who guides you; God Behind is the God who supports you; God to the Right is the God who accompanies you; God to the Left is the God who advises you; God in the Center is the God within you. Here again in an occult exercise we find ourselves coming close to prayer. One that is sometimes referred to as St. Patrick's Breastplate.

Evening Review

Because part of the sphere of occultism is the study of existence beyond death it can help us to perform in life some of the tasks that will confront us after death, and this is accomplished by a review of our past life. The stories of drowning men who have been saved describing their life passing before them is a small part of the review, which can also be an aspect of purgatory.

Therefore, as sleep is a lesser death, a useful exercise every evening on retiring to bed is to run through the event of the day, rather like a cine film, but backwards, from evening through till morning.

There is no need to pause or to make moral judgments about any part of the day's experiences but simply to run each one through. Doing it in reverse order will also be found to break up any persistent thought currents still churning round that so often lead to insomnia or bad dreams.

Withdrawal of Consciousness

Having performed the evening review, you should learn the correct withdrawal of consciousness from the physical vehicle and this may also be of assistance at the time of physical death. Simply start to withdraw life from your body, commencing with the feet, gradually moving it upwards until it is all in your head. This exercise is a technique for bridging the gap between lower and higher planes which exists by virtue of what

OCCULT EXERCISES AND PRACTICES

is theologically called the Fall.

The last two exercises, as they focus attention on the higher rather than the lower nature immediately before falling to sleep, are a potent means of self-development. The results are out of all proportion to the effort put into them, because the mind goes on working through the night in the direction in which it was upon falling asleep.

Therefore, to have your mind fixed upon the higher worlds rather than the problems or unfulfilled desires of the lower will result in greater soul growth and connection between the higher and lower aspects of the self.

This is not to discount entirely, however, the occasional use of the technique of deliberately 'sleeping upon a problem' in order to allow your subconscious mind to work upon it overnight with a view to a solution to the problem coming to you first thing in the morning.

Feeding the Mind

In preparation for the time when it has to deal with the intimations of higher consciousness, your concrete mind should be well stocked with images that can express some of the higher ideas. Accordingly, read up on plenty of mythology, for it is in the myths and legends of all races, particularly your own, that lie the images and archetypes which form the basis of communication of higher knowledge.

The exercise is a very enjoyable one and is worth doing for its own sake, as entertainment value and enrichment of the imagination, apart from any possible long-term esoteric effects. Easy-to-read children's books of the stories are often better than scholarly tomes in this respect.

It is largely the subconscious we wish to fill with the images, and the subconscious is no great scholar and cares little about niceties of scholarship. It just likes a good old-fashioned exciting read, with plenty of action and imagery.

Jungian psychology is also worth reading and modern fairy tales such as the *Lord of the Rings* trilogy and *The Silmarillion* by Tolkein.

Cosmological Books

Various cosmological books are also worth study, such as Dion Fortune's *Cosmic Doctrine*, H.P. Blavatsky's *Secret Doctrine*, Alice Bailey's *Treatises* on *Cosmic Fire*, *The Seven Rays* or *White Magic*, all of which are designed to train the mind as much as to inform it.

The very abstract concepts stretch the mental faculties, whether or not you believe what you read. The mere fact of trying to understand it is of esoteric value.

Science fiction should not be despised, as a means of mind stretching – and many a true word is written in high-flying speculation! Particularly in the works of C.S. Lewis, which also have theological dimensions (in particular, *That Hideaous Strength*).

Key Sentences

This exercise is a means of extracting the gist of a book or series of teachings and is meant to be applied in this context principally to occult books but can also be used in other study disciplines.

On reading through the book, attempt to select key

sentences which sum up whole sections or chapters. Underline them or write them down. This will provide you with material for meditation subjects and at the same time you will have extracted the book's essential message.

The Four Worlds

This is similar to the previous exercise, except that it is concerned, not with the written word, but with objects in daily life, all of which have an existence in the various levels of being, the lowest of which is the physical, the next being the formative, the next the creative, and the highest the archetypal.

For instance, a specific broom one observes is a physical object; brooms in general in all their variety from simple birch yard brooms to sophisticated vacuum cleaners are the formative level; the idea of sweeping or cleansing is the creative level; and the principle of purity is the archetypal seed.

This type of exercise, which should not be allowed to drift off into day-dreaming, is an excellent one for making a bridge between inner and outer in consciousness, which is of course one of the basic aims of occultism. One may also practice the exercise in reverse, by taking a principle and seeing in how many various ways it acts through the worlds to form different physical objects. The exercise is particularly valuable when done in regard to magical weapons particularly the sword, wand, cup, and pantacle or shield.

Divination

An important part of the mental training of an occult student is the development of the intuition; it is not always realized that many divination techniques are very much trainers of the intuition. The fortune-telling aspect, although perfectly valid, is usually over-emphasized and tends to cheapen and vulgarize a very delicate, accurate and highly intentioned technique of personal development.

The mechanism of most divinatory systems is to produce a model of the universe — using the word 'universe' in the sense of the immediate environment of any particular problem, however large or small.

Typical systems are the Tarot, which has 78 cards; or ordinary playing cards, of which there are 52, although sometimes a reduced pack is used. The Chinese system of the I Ching has 64 hexagrams derived from 16 trigrams, in turn derived from three sticks each of either positive or negative polarity.

The complex science of astrology has twelve zodiacal signs, twelve houses, ten planets, plus a few more abstract conceptions such as the Pars Fortuna, Cauda Draconis, etc. The less complex system of Geomancy has 16 symbols; whilst more homely systems such as reading the tea-cups depend upon the chance accumulation of an indeterminate but relatively small number of tea leaves.

It will be apparent that the more symbols there are, the more detailed or complex a reading, based upon the exercise of the intuition upon the complex pattern, will be possible. The 78 cards of the Tarot give more scope for subtlety and variation than the 16 dot-symbols of Geomancy; although it should be said that there is a personal factor involved and some will find they can work better with one system than another, whatever their intrinsic merits.

There are, indeed, other factors that come into play,

such as the position in which the symbols fall in relationship to one another. Thus if one had only four symbols, the number of ways they could be placed in sequence would be as many as twenty-four; five symbols would provide 120 possible combinations, and by the time one gets to ten symbols one is well into the millions of combinations.

Attitude of Mind
The attitude of mind in which divination is approached is very important and the following basic rules apply to all systems.

First, it must be approached in a spirit of absolute faith in the success of the operation, with a sincere desire to find out the truth, together with a sense of dedication and reverence for the fount of wisdom behind the oracle.

Thus there must never be a skeptical attitude of defying the oracle to prove itself. Nor should it be consulted in a light-hearted manner of 'doing it for a lark"or persistently demanding it to give answers to frivolous trivia. If one finds oneself in the position of saying to oneself 'What can we ask next?' — then don't ask anything — your attitude is wrong, which means that any answers are likely to be wrong also.

On the other hand, there should not be an atmosphere of fear of awesome portents. There must be a quiet and serene confidence. To this end, a short prayer or invocation to the power behind the oracle is often used. The form of words is not of detailed importance, as long as they express a sincere intention and respect for a source of wisdom, power and concern, greater than one's own.

Do not fall into the error of worshipping, or praying

Mental Exercises

to the oracle; this is idolatry. Rather, approach it as one would approach a wise old man. In consulting the I Ching it can help to visualize such a figure, a wise old Chinaman, not unlike Confucius. With the Tarot some people visualize an angelic figure (traditionally called HRU), but one could equally use a male or female figure based upon an appropriate Trump card — the Hermit, say, or the High Priestess.

Otherwise, a few minutes stilling the mind and contemplating the fact of a vast store of universal wisdom should be sufficient to get the mind into the required condition.

As in other types of occult exercise, it will also help if the same place is used, and the same time of day, for consulting the oracle. The implements of divination, be they cards, coins, stones or sticks, should be kept shut away when not in use and no one should be allowed to handle them idly, nor should they be used for any other purpose.

Formulating the Question

The second important rule is to formulate the question clearly. To ensure that this is done, even when reading for oneself (indeed especially when doing so), the question should be said aloud or written down. This will ensure that it is at least definite enough to be formulated into words and is not a nebulous wish or vague curiosity.

The next rule is to make the mind blank while shuffling or otherwise manipulating the implements. Many people will find this difficult to do, in which case they should endeavor to think solely about the question in hand — but without prejudging it. There should certainly be no irrelevant matters in the mind, or extraneous mood or emotions, and the spirit of dedicated inquiry should be maintained.

The fourth rule is an extension of this; to put all personal bias or preconceptions out of mind when consulting the oracle. This, too, is easier said than done, and is the main reason why divining for oneself is more difficult than doing it for others, even though, when reading for oneself, one has the advantage of knowing more about the general factors of the situation.

Finally, it is traditionally recommended that the same question should not be asked in the same day, certainly never within two hours, although matters arising from an earlier question can be followed up and clarified.

Safeguard Against Frivolous Use

Though cynics may say that this is to avoid showing that the oracle will give different answers to the same question because it is all a matter of chance anyway, the real purpose of this rule is to act as a safeguard against frivolous use. A hide-bound skeptic is unlikely ever to get a satisfactory answer anyway; his attitude of mind automatically cancels out the necessary rapport.

We are all for testing the validity of oracular methods, and far too little has been done upon this problem. It is unlikely that it will lend itself to strict laboratory conditions as expected by the disciplines of physical science. But, while having absolute faith at the time of making the reading, it is a valuable practice to keep careful note of the way the symbols felt and the interpretation that was placed upon them. Then to wait until time proves whether the answer was right or wrong, or inaccurate in certain respects. Such analysis after the event is a very good and necessary thing. And here skepticism is better than blind belief. But during the actual reading there must be belief and this is what the average scientific researcher generally fails to maintain.

The development of a scientific method of making, keeping and analyzing records is a sadly neglected thing. Yet it would help to establish the truth of this non-physical art and science and, moreover, be of considerable help to the student himself when he goes back over an old reading and finds he missed something important and failed to draw the right conclusions. That is, subsequent events prove the oracle right, but the interpretation wrong. There is no better school than this.

Note: For a more detailed look at divination using the Tarot cards, see *The Magical World of the Tarot* by Gareth Knight (Weiser).

OCCULT EXERCISES AND PRACTICES

CHAPTER FIVE

SPIRITUAL EXERCISES

Spiritual exercises are the simplest to speak about but the hardest to do. They are hard to do because they are not such well-defined objective practices as much occult work is, and also they strike right at the roots of one's being, so that indeed they may appear to be not so much exercises as counsels of perfection.

However, spiritual exercises are essential, and much is gained simply by the attempt to do them, even if one fails more often than one succeeds. In fact, the ability to 'fail right,' that is, to be able to accept the failure and try again, could be added to the list of spiritual exercises that follow here.

The ability to perform these exercises to the full will constitute proof of one's being an adept and master of life far more than any more spectacular abilities.

Harmlessness

The hallmark of the achieved human being is to be harmless, which does not mean being a weakling; it means having the correct attitude to all those about you and not indulging in malice, envy or fear, whether subjectively or objectively expressed. Remember that thoughts and feelings are as important as actions, for they have reality on their own level, and to be in the astral environment of someone who is in a suppressed fury can be every bit as horrifying as being trapped in a padded cell with a madman, however apparently civilized their overt behavior may be.

Resoluteness

An attribute of the human spirit is that it **IS** and in order to learn to express the spirit you should decide what you are going to do and then do it. Once a resolution is made it should be carried out — unless there are new facts which come to light which radically alter the correct appraisal of the situation.

This of course does not mean becoming hide-bound or a bigot. It is one of the difficulties of the spiritual exercises that each one has its hideous vice if incorrectly applied. The spiritual plane is not entirely a realm of sweetness and light, and still less the monopoly of the ineffectual.

Calmness

This is another hallmark of the person who is spiritually informed. It does not mean a cold aloofness nor feeble passivity but the ability to do things or to maintain poise without 'flapping' or dithering, or becoming a prey of indecision and lack of self-confidence.

Purity

The ultimate purity is purity of motive and thus you should examine all your actions to see just what your underlying motive is. 'The greatest treason is to do the right thing for the wrong reason' said T. S. Eliot's Thomas à Becket. This should not be the occasion for violent self-reproaches but simply a resolve to change the motive or action. Acceptance of what has occurred and the pursuit of remedial action without fuss is the true way to face faults, or 'sins,' to use an unfashionable word.

The repentance enjoined by the early Christian church meant in the original Greek simply a change of heart — not a wallowing self-abasement, which is but a perverted form of pride and self-righteousness.

The word 'purity,' has somehow become involved with sexual or other moral attitudes these days. Its true meaning refers to being unmixed or untainted with other things, and an idea of the importance of this is hinted at in the statement of a great one that 'if thine eye be single then thy body shall be full of light.'

Coordination

Many would-be occult students tend to lack coordination with their fellow human beings and the circumstances of daily life. And this applies also to those of even greater hidden spiritual ambition and pride, who will not enter into 'ordinary' human relationships and the responsibilities of life.

Every spiritually oriented person should be able to fit in with human society, to accept and be accepted, with no need to stand aside, cut off individually or as part of an 'in-group.'

The spirit is beyond such facile generalizations that express themselves in antipathy to race, class or creed, or to narrow-minded definitions such as 'suburban,'

OCCULT EXERCISES AND PRACTICES

'provincial,' 'arty,' 'Philistine,' 'bourgeois,' intellectual,' and so on.

Gratitude

The development of a sense of thankfulness for all the good things of life is a healthy spiritual virtue, and there are few who do not have many things to be thankful for. At its deepest level it becomes a thankfulness for whatever may befall, for even misfortune is capable of being transmuted by this type of spiritual alchemy, known commonly as 'thanksgiving.'

Steadfastness

This condition unites all the others we have mentioned, in being 'a light that does not flicker.' It indicates the way these spiritual exercises must be applied, at all times, by cultivation of a steady watchfulness over the different levels and actions of our own being.

This leads to self-identification as a spirit instead of being identified with one of the lower vehicles. So many are unconsciously identified with their mentality, their emotions, or their physical body. These should be tools or vehicles for the expression of the spirit, not usurpers of the rule of the spirit.

Nearness to God

The purpose of occult exercises is to open up awareness to other levels of existence beyond the physical plane. This takes time, just as it takes us a period of time as babies and children to learn the conditions of physical existence and cognition.

However, opening up consciousness and the ability to operate consciously upon higher planes does not automatically mean that you are becoming 'nearer to God'. God is present everywhere and can be approached as easily on the physical as on any other plane.

Confusion has arisen because much occultism stems from oriental sources, that regard God as high up and far away like a great potentate upon his throne. This was also a factor in medieval Jewish 'throne' mysticism, which is another source of modern occultism.

The thought that God is essentially high up and far away tends to lead to a belief that we can only approach him by means of various initiations and a process of learning to operate consciously upon the inner planes.

However, this process, valuable as it may be, has little to do with being near to God. What it does in fact is to integrate our own levels of being, but the 'god' we approach in this way is not so much the God of this Universe but the 'god' within the center of our own being, which should really be spelled with a small g.

The way to approach God is by means of prayer and a personal relationship with him on whatever plane of existence we may be considering.

Occultism and Religious Observance

It is by no means an ideal situation that there should be misunderstanding and suspicion between occultism and religion. Let us try to differentiate between them so that we can bring them together again in a true relationship.

At the present we often see a false relationship

OCCULT EXERCISES AND PRACTICES

whereby an occult school, in an endeavor to fit Christ into their scheme of things, comes close to becoming an off-beat religious sect. On the other hand there is often a rather dog-in-manger attitude of clergy who feel that occultists are making unwarranted, misguided and misinformed pronouncements about the faith.

What seems desirable is that there should be some within the church, whether they be priests or laymen makes no matter, who are capable of functioning consciously on all planes, as the occultist is trained to do.

And the corollary of this is that all occultists should take stock of their attitude to God, and this is best done through participation in any of the established religious denominations.

This may not be easy in the muddled heritage of confusion that exists in matters occult and matters religious. Many naturally religious people have been repelled by a strictly religious upbringing — and 'Christian education' of the narrower sort has much to answer for in the lack of practicing religion in adulthood.

Let us simply state that the exercises in this book are no substitute for religious practices. They are concerned with our own development or education, and are thus in a true sense scientific rather than devotional. We miss a very great deal if we attempt to throw over a personal relationship with God and try to hoist ourselves up to heaven by our own boot straps.

Five Types of Prayer

Very briefly, prayer consists of thinking of God our

Creator, and the Creator of the world in which we live, and this can be done in five main ways.

1. When we think of God in his holiness our prayer is one of *adoration*;

2. When we think of how our achievement falls so far below the glory of God and example of Christ our prayer is one of *contrition*;

3. When we think of the good things we have to be thankful to God for, our prayer is one of *thanksgiving*;

4. When we look forward to receiving more good things from God our prayer is one of *supplication*;

5. When we look forward to such good things for others our prayer is one of *intercession*.

We should not let the sun go down without at least one form of prayer or another and no one can possibly achieve the heights of occult development without a lively personal relationship with God. Indeed, without God occult practice can be a snare and a delusion.

Spiritual Training Systems

There are two main methods of spiritual teaching, or mystical approaches to God: the *via positiva* or Positive Way, and the *via negativa* or Negative Way. They are so-called because the first uses symbols as an approach to inner realities, while the latter — on the

OCCULT EXERCISES AND PRACTICES

grounds that any material symbol must be an inaccurate representation of a transcendent reality — uses no symbols at all.

And the corollary is indeed true, that the devotional mystics who have a lively relationship with their personal God — with the living Christ — have no need of occultism for the safety and salvation of their souls. They have their own particular and specialized vocation.

Two small classic treatises stand out as examples of each way. *The Spiritual Exercises* of St. Ignatius of Loyola represents the positive way, and *The Cloud of Unknowing* by an anonymous fourteenth-century English mystic, represents the negative way.

The Ignatian method is similar in its initial approaches to the techniques of the active imagination found in occult astral exercises. Selected scenes are taken from the Bible and one imagines oneself taking part in them as a preliminary to a heart-to-heart communion with God. One could equally take other devotional works as a starting point such as Dante's *Divine Comedy* which is, in fact, a complete curriculum of spiritual development couched in the language and with the viewpoint of the High Middle Ages.

The method of *The Cloud* is more akin to mantra yoga, the centering of the mind upon a single phrase, or in this case a single word, that represents or is addressed to God. A slightly less rigorous method is found in the 'Jesus Prayer' of the Orthodox Church, which consists of the repetition, with conviction, of the formula 'Lord Jesus Christ, Son of God, have mercy upon me, a sinner,' often, as with occult astral and mental exercises, to the accompaniment of rhythmic breathing. The words of the Jesus Prayer are held, by its advocates, to contain or imply the essentials of spiritual truth and Christian belief.

The Imitation of Christ

Perhaps the best formulation of a devotional system that comprises all the foregoing is the fifteenth-century treatise by Thomas a Kempis, *The Imitation of Christ*. Thomas was very much a Christian initiate and his book is of such mystical power that even the reading of it can act as a spiritual stimulation and protection from the forces of darkness.

OCCULT EXERCISES AND PRACTICES

APPENDIX

PSYCHIC SELF-DEFENCE

Personal Magnetism

The practice of personal magnetism is looked at somewhat askance by some as an attempt to dominate others by the will. However, in everyday life it really does nothing of the kind, for it is simply a technique for strengthening the personality and holding one's own in personal relationships. And many people, particularly psychic ones, need all the help they can get in meeting others on equal terms. Others can quite easily dominate them, often without realizing it, for the psychic who does too much psychic work can develop into a very passive type of personality.

An important part of personal magnetism is to be relaxed and to concentrate on remaining relaxed. You can assume a positive mental attitude by building up an image of the person you are to meet beforehand and taking up a positive attitude towards *that*. Then in the presence of the actual person it is a question of looking them firmly in the eyes when important points are being made.

The eyes do play an important part in this and they can be strengthened by practice of gazing or staring at an object without allowing the gaze to wander, or blinking too much.

It is important of course at the same time when looking at a person, to throw your will into your gaze. Not of course in a fixed or hypnotic manner, but with the confident expectation that the person is likely to agree with you.

Posture also plays an important part in all this, particularly the aids already mentioned in regard to opening and closing the aura to psychic influence.

Physical Defense

We may of course meet people who are strong personalities and given to using these techniques in an aggressive manner, and there are defences against them. Such people can be very objectionable and should someone look at you fixedly, trying to impose their will, then simply gaze at a point between their eyebrows and you may then stare them out of countenance quite simply and without effort. But do not let them fix you in the eyes with their own.

Astral Defence

An astral method is to imagine a very thick sheet of plate glass between you and the other person, or perhaps a brick wall, or even moving cutting edges.

A person known to the author, who was known to dominate by visualizing a thread connecting his own brow center to the mind of another, was successfully repulsed by his victim imagining whirling lawn mower

Appendix

blades cutting the thread. The aggressor never tried it again. This particular defense has the advantage that it is easier to imagine a moving object than a static one.

A sphere of blue light all around you is an excellent defense method, or you can imagine a blue cloak. A good dodge is to work out a ritual gesture of putting on a cloak and flicking the hood over your head. A little ingenuity and practice will demonstrate that this can be quite easily done in the form of a gesture which passes in ordinary society as a kind of half shrug or stretch.

Although these exercises have their place, the real strength should come from a higher level through becoming open to your own higher forces, which are developed in the mental exercises in this book. And also by faith — which comes through prayer.

In all these cases the sign that all is under control is that of complete physical relaxation, therefore this point should be watched and maintained all the while. If you can simply maintain physical relaxation in difficult circumstances, this is more than half the battle.

Occult Attack

Influencing people at a distance, even when beyond visual range, by techniques of clairvoyance is often a worry to those new to occultism through the influence of popular occult novels or films.

There is, however, much exaggeration over the misuse of these skills, because the effort required in most cases far exceeds any possible result in terms of physical gain, even if a genuine motive exists.

OCCULT EXERCISES AND PRACTICES

Having a good meal or watching a comic video is sufficient exorcism or means of controlling your imagination against most risks of this kind.

Pixley Exercises

Finally, from the system of visualization exercises devised by Olive Pixley, we include an excellent general purpose protective exercise which can be performed at any time, particularly in the face of emergencies. Instead of trying to 'brace' yourself against a crisis, the 'taking on' of the Name will induce a true equilibrium so that whatever the emergency, you will spontaneously do and say the right thing.

The Name is pronounced Deay-Thu-Th. DE is just the sound of the letter D, and AY rhymes with 'nay.' THU is pronounced as in 'coo,' and TH as in 'that.'

The first syllable DEAY (which represents equilibrium in matter) is in the shape of a triangle of vivid deep blue light. It is flashed down at the back of the head on the right-hand side, starting just above it. It runs along the nape of the neck and flashes back to the point above the right side of the head. It is brought down on a deep outbreath to the sound of Deay-ay-ay, forming a right-angled triangle.

The next syllable THU (which represents perfect receptivity) is also in vivid blue light but in the shape of a chalice on the top of the head. Form it on a deep inbreath, and know that you will receive all the Light that you can.

TH is a very soft sound on an outbreath (It is perfect transmission and givingness). It is a flash of Light that comes through the head, flashes through the body, and ends in the left side in a spiral movement forwards, and feels like a pulse.

Appendix

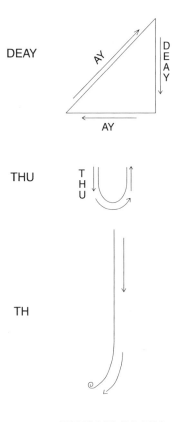

DEAY THU TH

To resume, DEAY-AY-AY is on a strong outbreath. THU on an inbreath. TH on a soft outbreath. Deay-thu-th is the Aramaic form of the name Jesus, Aramaic being the language spoken by Our Lord and the disciples.

The Name Exercise, in the above form, gives the ability to tune in to the three aspects of perfection necessary to perfect manifestation in the world, namely Equilibrium, Receptivity and Transmission. These it is easy to align with the three Pillars of Qabalistic

OCCULT EXERCISES AND PRACTICES

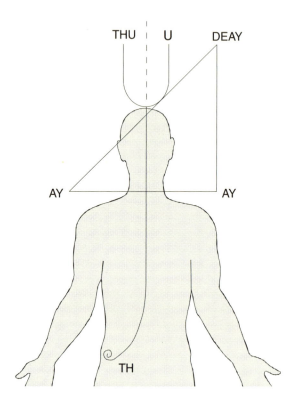

teaching. Just as the Christian religion is a development from the ancient Hebrew religion as presented in the Old Testament, so is esoteric Christianity a development from the ancient Jewish Mystery Tradition, the Qabalah.

The Name Exercise has other uses. In another form it can be used as a help and protection for others, or over houses, trains, boats, cars, airplanes, etc. It can be used to resolve differences and disharmonies between friends, relatives, neighbors or others, or for the smooth functioning of committees and conferences. Or in a wider sense it may be used for the help of the world generally.

Appendix

Further details of the Name Exercise may be found together with a number of similar exercises in Olive Pixley's *Armour of Light* – available from:

The Council of The Technique in Light
Mr. Peter F. Harris
58 High Street
Burford, Oxfordshire
OX18 4QF
England

OCCULT EXERCISES AND PRACTICES

Index

Adept, 8, 71
Adepts, 50
Adoration, 77
Aether, 27-29
Ajna, 30
Alchemy, 74
Alphabet, 48
Anatomy, 25
Antakarana, 59
Aquarian Age, 4
Aramaic Name of Christ, 85
Archetypes 8, 36, 45, 62, 64
Astrology, 65
Atonement, 9
Aura, 18, 25-26, 40, 57, 82
Autosuggestion, 52
Awareness, 9, 14-15, 53, 59, 74
Banishing, 21, 34
Bible, 8, 78
Breath, 12-13, 25-26
Calmness, 72
Cauda draconis, 65
Cave, 36
Centers, 30
Ceremonial, 60
Chakras, 30
Chalice, 4, 21, 84
Christ, 45, 76-79
Christian, 73, 76, 78-79, 86
Christianity, 86
Church, 58, 73, 76, 78
Churches, 17, 40
Clairvoyance, 83
Clergy, 76
Color, 14, 26, 28, 30
Communion, 78
Complementaries, 30
Conjuring, 31
Contacts, 36
Contemplation, 29
Coordination, 73
Courage, 53
Creation, 60
Creator, 77
Creed, 73
Cross, 21, 25, 33, 40, 60
Crystal Gazing, 46
Cube, 20, 23
Cube of Space 60
Cup, 64
Dabblers, 48
Dance, 22, 39
Dancing, 36
Daydreaming, 64
Death, 54-55, 61
De-ay-thuth, 84-85
Depression, 40
Desires, 62
Devotion 78-79

OCCULT EXERCISES AND PRACTICES

Divination, 8, 64-69
Dodecahedron, 20, 22
Doorway, 36, 52
Dreams, 44, 61
Dusk, 14
Dying, 54
Eastern systems, 7, 12, 16, 27-30, 39, 58
Elements, 20-21, 27, 29-30
Emotions, 18, 21-22, 39-40, 68, 74
Equilibrium, 39, 84-85
Esotericists, 57
Evening Review, 61
Evil, 8-9
Evocation, 34
Exorcism, 84
Faculties, inner, 9, 33, 46
Fairies, 36, 63
Faith, 8, 31, 66, 68, 76, 83
Fear, 53, 66, 72
Feelings, 14, 21, 38, 72
Fiction, 35, 63
Films, 83
Fingers, 12, 17, 19, 27, 39, 50
Flapping, 72
Flashing tablets, 27, 29-30
Flowers, 41, 45
Folly, 8, 37
Forces, 18, 21, 25-26, 79, 83
Fortuna, 65
Fortunetelling, 65
Fourfold breath, 13
Fraternities, 43
Frivolous use of oracles, 68
Geomancy, 65
Geometry, 27, 49
Gestures, 39-40
Givingness, 84
Gods, 17
God within, 9
Grace, 24
Grail, 20
Gratitude, 74
Groups, 8
Guardian, 45
Guidance, 48
Guide Meditation, 35-36

Guides, 60
Gustatory suggestion, 41
Handicrafts, 18
Harmlessness, 71
Hazel, 47
Healing, 8, 25-26, 37-38
Health, 38
Heart, 43, 49, 60, 73
Heaven, 31, 76
Heavens, 59
Hebrew, 86
Hermit, 67
Hexagrams, 65
Hierophant, 45
Holiness, 77
Hru, 67
Hygiene, 33
I Ching, 65, 67
Icosahedron, 20
Identification, 45
Idolatry, 67
Imitation of Christ, 79
Impressions, 49-50
Incense, 24, 40, 41
Initiate, 79
Initiations, 75
Insomnia, 61
Integration, 18
Intelligences, 45
Intercession, 77
Intuition, 8, 21, 59, 64-65
Invocation, 45, 66
Jesus, 78, 85
Jewels, 38
Joss sticks, 41
Jungian psychology, 21, 60, 63
Jupiter, 38
Justice, 38
Kneeling, 16-17
Knowledge, 18, 45, 62
Language, 24, 39, 78, 85
Legends, 45, 62
Logic, 19
Love, 38
Magic, 8, 21, 24-26, 51, 60, 63
Magnetism, 81

Index

Mandala, 21, 60
Mantras, 34, 78
Memory, 41-42, 44
Mercury, 38
Mercy, 78
Minerals, 47
Mnemonics, 42
Modeling, 20, 22, 24, 39
Models, 19-20
Moon, 38
Moralizing, 37
Mysticism, 75, 77, 78, 79
Mythology, 59, 62
Myths, 62
Names, 34
Nets, 23
Novels, 83
Octahedron, 20
Olfactory suggestion, 40-41
Optical illusions, 28, 30
Oracles, 64-69
Ouija board, 48
Pantacle, 64
Passivity, 72
Pendulum, 47-48
Pentagram, 21
Perceptions, 15
Perfection, 71, 85
Perseverance, 46
Personality, 19, 81
Philosophy, 21, 31
Pillars, 52, 85
Planes, 8-9, 61, 75-76
Planetary attributions, 37-38
Platonic solids, 20, 22-23
Playing, 22, 37, 65
Polarity, 65
Postures, 16-18
Powers, 12, 14
Prayer, 40, 76-77
Pride, 73
Priestess, 67
Priests, 76
Projection, 18, 45, 51-52
Projections, 36
Protection, 79, 84-86

Psychism, 8, 57
Psychology, 21, 60, 63
Psychometry, 50
Purgatory, 61
Purity, 31, 64, 72-73
Pythagoras, 20
Qabalah, 86
Reason, 68, 73
Recalling past lives, 53
Receptivity, 84-85
Recollection, 59-60
Relationships, 19, 38, 73, 81
Relax, 11-14
Religion, 75-76, 86
Repentance, 73
Resoluteness, 72
Reverence, 66
Rhymes, 84
Safety, 78
Salutation, midday, 59-60
Saturn, 38
Sectarianism, 8
Seership, 57
Self-abasement, 73
Self-confidence, 53, 72
Self-deception, 37
Self-hypnosis, 52
Self-identification, 74
Self-projection, 51
Self-righteousness, 8, 73
Sentimentality, 19
Shell Hearing, 46-47
Sleep, 43-44, 53, 61-62
Solar, 17, 25, 37-38, 60
Sorcery, 8
Soul, 24, 43, 62
Spine, 17-18
Spirits, 39
St Patrick's Breatplate, 61
Stability, 38
Star, 21
Stars, 38
Steadfastness, 74
Stonehenge, 43
Stones, 43, 67
Stories, 61-62

OCCULT EXERCISES AND PRACTICES

Suggestion, 40-41
Sun, 4, 21, 36, 38, 59-60, 77
Super-conscious, 45
Sword, 64
Symbol, 21, 28-29, 35-36, 38-39, 43, 78
Symbolism, 7, 20-21, 28, 37
Talismans, 38, 51
Tarot, 35-36, 65, 67, 69
Tattvas, 22, 27-29
Tea Leaves, reading, 65
Telepathy, 49-50
Temple, 20, 43
Tetrahedron, 20
Thankfulness, 74
Thanksgiving, 74, 77
Thaumaturgy, 8
Three-dimensional models, 18-19, 60

Trance, 52-53
Trigrams, 65
Trilithons, 43
Unconscious, 11-12, 37
Universe, 15, 37, 44, 65, 75
Unknowing, 78
Venus, 38
Visualization, 12, 26, 35, 39, 42, 51, 84
Wand, 47, 64
Watchfulness, 74
Wine, 41
Worshipping, 66
Yoga, 18, 39, 78
Zen, 15-16
Zodiac, 22, 37, 65

For information on additional titles, write:

SUN CHALICE BOOKS
PO Box 9703
Albuquerque, New Mexico
USA 87119